God's
little book of
Comfort

Words to soothe and
reassure in troubled times

Richard Daly

Collins

Collins, a division of
HarperCollins Publishers
77–85 Fulham Palace Road

First published in Great Britain in 2008
© 2008 HarperCollins

Richard Daly asserts the moral right to be identified as the author
of this work

A catalogue record for this book is available from the British
Library

ISBN-13: 978-0-00-727838-1

1

Printed and bound in Great Britain
by Martins the Printers Ltd, Berwick upon Tweed
Typeset by MATS Typesetters, Southend-on-Sea, Essex

INTRODUCTION

One of the basic needs for all humanity
is to be comforted in times of personal sorrow
or difficulty. Many times that comfort can come
through words of support and encouragement
from special people in our lives. However,
there are times when we need more, especially
in times of need. God is the one who is able
to supply all our needs and promises
us that if we call on Him,
He will be there for us.

God offers comfort to all who are willing
to come to him. The invitation is extended
to everyone.

Jesus says in Matthew 11:28
*'Come unto me all you who labour and are heavy
laden and I will give you rest.'*

This rest is not a temporary fix but
a permanent solution;
it is a complete rest for the soul.

This little book is designed
to help you get in tune with this God of comfort
and to lead you more fully to the one who is our
'very present help in time of trouble.'

REPLENISH YOURSELF

It's in the 'valleys' of your life that
you can drink from God's sweetest
streams. It's during this
period when He restores your soul.

Jeremiah 30:17
Psalm 51:12

RESPECT YOURSELF

God tells us to 'love our neighbours as we
love ourselves.' To love yourself simply means
appreciating who you are in Christ.

Mark 12:33
Psalm 139:14

OVERDO IT

Find something to laugh about; a past
memory or incident and
laugh so that loud your face hurts!

Genesis 21:6

TREASURE PLEASANT MOMENTS

Isn't it comforting when you're lying
in bed listening to the rain outside? Next
time it happens, treasure the feeling!

Psalm 37:4

LET GOD LEAD

No matter what you're going
through today, you can count on God
to be with you – you can be sure He'll
bring you through.

Isaiah 49:14-16

LIVE TO YOUR CONSCIENCE

Comfort comes in knowing you've done the
right thing, no matter what people think.

2 Kings 22:2

WATCH WHERE YOU'RE HEADING

'Some people are so fond of ill-luck that
they run half-way to meet it.'

Douglas W. Jerrold

Psalm 18:10

BE ASSURED

'Where there is sorrow there is holy ground.'

Oscar Wilde

Isaiah 35:10

FIND THE LESSON

Whatever despairing situation you may find
yourself in, the important question to ask is,
'Lord, what do you want me to learn
from this experience?'

Job 13:15

DISCOVER GOD'S PLAN

The reason God has brought you through
so much is because He has a unique and specific
purpose for your life. Get into His presence
and discover what it is.

John 15:26
Jeremiah 29:11

APPRECIATE THE STRUGGLE

Read Hebrews chapter 11. It contains many of
God's heroes…Yet everyone of them had
their struggles. God can use your struggles
to make you strong.

Hebrews 11:34

DISCOVER YOUR WEAKNESS

Your limitations are God's opportunities
to get you to depend on Him. In God's eyes they
serve a divine purpose.

1Peter 1:7
Proverbs 17:3
Isaiah 48:10

WHAT ARE YOU THINKING?

'Nothing is miserable unless you think it so.'

De Consolatione Philosophaie

Proverbs 23:7

DEVELOP A POSITIVE OUTLOOK

Your attitude determines your behaviour.
You choose whether to be happy or sad, thankful
or grumpy. Choose a positive outlook today!

Ephesians 5:20
Amos 4:5

SOAK IT AWAY

Next time you're feeling low – run a nice hot
bath, pour in your favourite bubble bath and salts
and soothe away your worries.

Jeremiah 51:8

LET GOD IN

God is personally interested in you. He wants
you to include Him in all your areas of your life.
If you do, your plans will prosper.
What you plant will produce fruit.

Proverbs 3:6
Proverbs 16:3
Deuteronomy 8:18

MOVE FORWARD

You are as close to God as you
want to be. The more you draw near to God
the more he will draw near to you.

James 4:8

MAKE THE RIGHT CHOICE

What you are today was determined by
the decisions of yesterday. If you want to
change your future, learn how to make
better decisions today.

Joshua 24:15

DON'T WORRY

Anxiety paralyses you and takes away everything good in your life. Don't let it take control, otherwise you'll end up immobilised.

Philippians 4:6-7
Psalm 56:3
Matthew 6:31-33

WHEN GOD CALLS... MOVE

When God unexpectedly moves you to speak
words of comfort to somebody – do it.
It's about God's timing not yours.

Proverbs 11:30

LET GO

When you can't understand – TRUST!

Deuteronomy 29:29

STOP AND LISTEN

In the business of your daily routine
remember God has a word for you. Be still...and
let God be God in your life.

Psalm 46:10

APPRECIATE YOUR UNIQUENESS

God's love for you is unlimited. If you were
the only person that needed forgiveness,
Jesus would have
gone to the cross just for you.

1 John 4:18

COME TO DADDY

'Abba Father' is an expression given to
God. It means literally 'my daddy'…That's how
intimate he wants us to be with Him.
How wonderful!

Romans 8:15

IT'S NOT BY CHANCE

You're not here today because you're
lucky. You're here today because you're
blessed! Take a moment to thank God.

1Peter 5:7

YOUR CHANCE SHALL COME

'For the Lord himself shall descend from
Heaven…and we shall be caught up
to meet the Lord in the air and so shall
we ever be with the Lord. Therefore comfort
one another with these words.'

1 Thessalonians 4:17-18

ACCEPT CHRIST'S INVITATION

In times of burnout, Christ offers us a
permanent solution. He says, 'Come unto
me all you who labour and are heavy burdened
and I will give you rest.'

Matthew 11:28-29
Hebrews 4:9

CONSIDER YOURSELF INVALUABLE

In God's eyes your mistakes don't make
you a failure, for in Christ you are
always a success.

Romans 8:38

CONSIDER YOUR TROUBLES
WORTHWHILE

Whatever you may be going through, remember
what you suffer now will be nothing compared
to the glory He will give you later.

Romans 8:18

BACK TO THE FUTURE

Jesus is the same yesterday, today and forever.
You can't go back, but He can. He can heal
your wounded past and break chains
that had you bound.

Hebrews 13:8
Isaiah 65:17

BE TRANSFORMED BY THE TRANSFORMER

God is not content with your status quo.
Every day in countless ways he seeks to mould
and develop you into a greater likeliness
of His son.

Ephesians 4:1

KEEP YOUR EYES HEAVENWARD

Don't focus on the mountains that
come up before you, rather focus on the
mountain-mover. Nothing is too hard for him.

Mark 11:23-24

BE PATIENT IN TRIALS

With God, waiting is not wasted time.
When you wait on the Lord,
He will renew your strength.

Psalm 37:34

FOLLOW GOD'S WAY

God can turn your rejection to redirection.
When one door is closed, He will always open
another. Watch out for it.

Revelation 3:8

CLAIM GOD'S ETERNAL LOVE

God's compassion towards you never fails.
Each morning there is a renewed supply. When
you woke up you were surrounded by a fresh
outpouring of His love.

Lamentations 3:22-23

CONSIDER YOURSELF SECURED

When you seek God's protection, nothing
can get to you without first coming
through Him.

Isaiah 54:57

EXPLORE GOD'S BENEFITS

God has encouraging words you've never heard,
places you've never been and joys you've never
experienced. Let Him lead you
today.

Proverbs 4:18

DON'T GIVE UP

When it looks like there's no way forward
for you, don't stop short
of the prize. The greater the conflict, the greater
the conquest. The stronger the battle,
the sweeter the victory.

2 Chronicles 20:15
1 Samuel 17:47

LOOK FOR GOD'S PROVIDENCE

No matter how bad things may
look today, His word to you is:
'The Lord Himself goes before you and will
be with you. Do not be afraid. Do not
be discouraged.'

Deuteronomy 31:8

CARPE DIEM!

Seize the day! Appreciate the 'now'
moments of you life.
Once passed they will never
return.

Ephesians 5:16

SEEK GOD FIRST

Too often we talk to everybody
about our problems, except the one
who can do something about it.
God says 'let your requests be
made known unto me.'

Philippians 4:6

INVOLVE GOD

When the picture looks bleak, don't ask
God to take you out of it, but to join you in it.
That way everything is transformed, including you.

Mark 4:39

DON'T STAY DOWN

Proverbs talks about a righteous person who
may fall down seven times but always gets back
up again. You can be knocked down but
never knocked out!

Proverbs 24:16
Corinthians 4:8-9
Psalm 37:24

SEE WEAKNESS AS STRENGTH

It's when you are at your weakest,
that God is able to make you a person
of power.

2 Corinthians 12:9

BELIEVE GOD

Don't fret about what other people
think of you. What God thinks is what
counts.

Zechariah 2:8

TAKE THE FIRST STEP

If you take a thousand steps away from
God, you only have to turn around towards Him.
He's been following you all
the way.

Luke 15:4
Luke 19:10

LIVE JOYFULLY

Happy people rarely tend to think
about happiness. They're too busy
living it.

Proverbs 16:20

SEEK POWER IN PRAYER

'Seven days without prayer, makes one weak.'

Anon

James 5:13-16

LET GOD FILL YOU

God gives spiritual food
to everyone – except those who
are full of themselves.

Proverbs 16:18

ACCEPT GOD'S VIEW

You would worry less about
what others think of you
if you realised how seldom they do.
Respect God's good opinion.

Psalm 139:17-18

PASS ON THE BATON

To be appreciated
is among the deepest cravings of
human nature. When you have received it,
dish it out to someone else.

Hebrews 13:1
John 15:12

GOD'S PLAN CAN'T FAIL

With God there's no such thing as a
'Mission Impossible'. When He sends you
on a mission, He makes sure you
have the means to succeed.

Luke 1:37

YOU'RE ALWAYS ON GOD'S MIND

God will never ever forget you. Your very
name is engraved on the palm of His hand.

Isaiah 49:16

KEEP GOING

It's when the burden seems
heaviest, that the breakthrough is near.
Hold on for it.

Galatians 6:9

TAKE TIME OUT

When you're under pressure – that's the time
to snatch a few moments to pause and relax,
reflecting on the goodness of life.

Psalm 46:10
Mark 1:35

KEEP TRUSTING

There is a rainbow in the soul
for every storm that comes your way.
Faith is the assurance that the sun will
shine again.

2 Chronicles 20:20

FOLLOW THE LIGHT

God's word makes it clear
that the way of the cross
will sometimes bring sacrifice, suffering and
loss. But He promises also to walk by
our side as our light for the journey.

Matthew 10:39

DON'T FORGET YOUR BLESSINGS

Treasure the memories of all God
has done in the past – bring them to
mind as beacons of hope for the
future.

Jeremiah 31:3-4

BE STILL

The Lord will not shout to get
your attention. It's up to you to
get away from the world's distractions
to quiet your soul and listen closely to His
still, small voice.

Isaiah 30:15

BASK IN GOD'S PRESENCE

In the shadow of doubt
in the depths of despair
in the struggle for hope
be assured God is there.

Genesis 28:15

CONFESS YOUR SINS

The same crucified Christ who said
'Father forgive them for they know
not what they do' is the same Christ
who opens His arms wide with forgiveness
for you too.

Psalm 103:12

YOU'RE WORTH IT!

The Lord doesn't see you as
useless or unworthy – to Him you're not
helpless. You were worth Calvary's cross.

Psalm 13:5

TURN SORROW INTO JOYFULNESS

Out of difficulties grow miracles.
Your disappointments are God's appointments.

Psalm 30:11

APPRECIATE WHO YOU ARE

Don't compare yourself with others.
There are always greater and lesser people
than yourself. Value who you are in Christ.

Romans 8:17
1 Peter 2:9

YOU ARE WHO YOU ARE

You are unique. There is no one
who is exactly the same as you. You are
one of a kind, special, original and valued by God.

Jeremiah 1:5

DON'T THROW IN THE TOWEL

Being defeated is only a temporary condition. It's when you give up that it becomes permanent.

Matthew 24:13
James 1:12
2 Timothy 2:3

KEEP PRESSING ON

Striving toward your potential ought to be
your purpose in life.

Ecclesiastes 9:10

LOOK FOR THE WAY OUT

Remember, you will never be faced with
a temptation that is too hard
for you to resist.

1 Corinthians 10:13
2 Peter 2:9

WAIT ON THE LORD

A comforting thought is that no
evil will last forever or indeed for very long.
Whatever the trial... 'it too shall pass.'

2 Corinthians 4:17
1 Corinthians 15:52

KEEP YOUR COOL

Keeping your head when everyone around
you is losing theirs is an example
of peace.

Isaiah 26:3
Galatians 5:22

FACE THE FEAR

'Not everything that is faced
can be changed, but nothing
can be changed until it is faced.'

James Baldwin

Philippians 4:13

BUILD UP YOUR RESISTANCE

Tough times do not last.
Tough people do!

2 Timothy 2:3

LOOK AT YOURSELF

'The most difficult matter is
not so much to change the world
as yourself.'

Nelson Mandela

Mark 8:36

MAKE THE MOST OF LIFE

'Things work out best for
people who make the best of
the way things work out.'

John Woode

Philippians 4:11
Hebrews 13:5

REMEMBER THE POSITIVES

Count your blessings - not your troubles.

Philippians 4:8

VALUE LOVED ONES

The special people God has
placed in your life today are there for a
reason. Treasure them moment by moment.

Proverbs 17:17

YOU'RE A WINNER

To lose is not to fail. The
only failure is to lose and not
try again. With Jesus you can never fail.

Proverbs 8:37

PRAY THE SERENITY PRAYER

'God grant me the serenity to
accept the things I cannot change; the courage
to change the things I can, and the wisdom
to know the difference.'

Anonymous

James 1:5
Proverbs 4:5

MAKE THE MOST OF NOW

'To dream of the person you
would like to be is to waste
the person you are.'

Anonymous

Ephesians 5:20

ASK FOR POWER

Instead of asking for an easier life
ask God to make you a stronger person.

Isaiah 40:29
Psalm 29:11

LET GO, LET GOD

To cast your burdens on the
Lord means letting go and trusting God
for your next step forward.

Psalm 22:10
Proverbs 4:18

LET GOD LEAD

There are no hopeless situations. In every
misfortune God always has a way out for you.
Just hold his hand.

2 Samuel 22:31
Job 23:10

GET UP!

It's OK to be down in
the dumps. Just don't stay there too long.

2 Samuel 12:22-23.

GIVE IT YOUR ALL

When you know you've done your
best, God can't ask of you anything more.

Ecclesiastes 9:10

BELIEVE GOD'S TRUTH

Sometimes we suffer more in
imagination than reality.
Bring your thoughts in line with the truth.

Proverbs 23:7
Psalm 117:2
James 3:14

LOOK FOR THE SILVER LINING

If there were no clouds
we wouldn't appreciate when the
sun comes out.

Matthew 5:45

DON'T LET FEAR STOP YOU

Sometimes in order to overcome a weakness,
even though you may feel the fear, persevere
and do it 'afraid' anyhow.

Proverbs 3:25-26

MAKE THE BEST OF THE SITUATION

You can't control the cards life
deals you, but you can control how you
decide to play them.

Proverbs 3:5-6

LET GOD PRUNE YOU

The pruning process can be a painful
one, but God knows what needs to be cut
back in your life. Trust Him with the knife.

John 15:2

TURN FAILURE INTO SUCCESS

Some people grow through failure; others
never recover from it. See your mistakes
as stepping stones rather than stumbling blocks.

Proverbs 24:16

DON'T STAY DOWN

You must be like the lady who
said, 'I'm never down, I'm either up or
getting up!' Are you going to get up and
try again?

Psalm 130:4

YOU'RE A NEW CREATION

The moment you accept God's forgiveness
you no longer 'have a dark past'. You
have a bright future.

Philippians 3:13
Psalm 51

BE ANXIOUS FOR NOTHING

Jesus said 'Can all your worries
add a single moment to your life?' Of
course not! Worry changes nothing.

Matthew 6:27

REACH THE NEXT LEVEL

God not only wants to forgive you
of your sins – He also wants to cleanse you,
heal you, restore you and give you
complete victory.

1 John 1:7
Proverbs 28:13

GET YOUR DIPLOMA OF VICTORY

As difficult as it may be, you are in
your present position for a reason. But you are
only there for a season. Take the tests, graduate
and move on to what God has next.

2 Corinthians 4:17

LET GOD WORK IT OUT

For those who love the Lord, no
experience is ever wasted… 'all things work
together for good to those who love God, to those
who are called according to His promises.'

Romans 8:28

GET FREE IN CHRIST

Unforgiveness creates a yoke that you
carry around wherever you go.
The power of forgiveness sets you free

Matthew 5:25

TUNE INTO THE MASTER

God never changes. If He spoke to
people in the Bible, He will speak
to you too. Take time out to recognise His voice.

Revelation 3:20
John 10:4

ENJOY YOURSELF

To be content is to announce 'I am
what I am. I cannot be anything other
than what God has called me. So I will be the
best me I can be. I will enjoy each day of me.'

John 3:27

PATIENCE IS A VIRTUE

Waiting is not easy, but it is necessary.
God is working on both ends of the line;
He's getting you ready for 'it' and He is
getting 'it' ready for you.

Habakkuk 2:3

HANG IN THERE

When you finally decide to let something go
you may feel empty for a time. This is
normal. You are in between pain and the peace
that will come.

Revelation 3:11
James 1:3

REPLENISH YOURSELF

Stop regularly to recall God's
goodness. It restores your perspective and
strengthens you to face what's ahead.

Psalm 69:30

YOU'RE INVINCIBLE WITH GOD

If God is with us who can be
against us? The presence of God tilts
the scales forever in your direction.

Romans 8:31

THE FOUR-LETTER WORD

Things getting you down? Too tired to pray?
Let me suggest one of a few four-letter
words God loves to hear us use...HELP!

Jeremiah 33:3

GO BACK TO BASICS

When was the last time you flew a kite, took a long walk in the woods, peddled a bike, or just watched the sun set?

Ecclesiastes 12:1

INCLINE YOUR EARS TO HIM

God is trying to tell you to be
quiet, be still and listen. Then, to move over
so He can take control.

Job 14:14
Psalm 40:1
Habakkuk 2:3

REST IN HIS ARMS

God says, 'I will hold you up', as long as you
continue to lean on Him.

Proverbs 3:4-5

TRUST IN GOD

Worry is incompatible with faith.
They just don't mix. Through the events
of life one has to give.

Hebrews 10:23
James 1:6

STOP THE LEAK

Refuse to allow
tomorrow's lagoon of worries to drain
into today's lake. If not you end up flooded.

Matthew 6:25-33

LIVE DAILY

Take one day at a time. That's the
way God dispenses life. He knows what will
work together for good.

Psalm 118:24
Proverbs 27:1

DOWN BUT NOT OUT

When you find yourself fallen down, you're
already in the best position to reach out to God...
on your knees.

Psalm 145:14
Psalm 37:24

CHERISH THE UNPREDICTABLE

'The only certainty is that nothing is certain.'

Pliny the Elder

Psalm 103:15-17

TRUST AND OBEY

Leaving the details of your future
in God's hands is one of the most honourable
acts of obedience you can do.

Psalm 37:5

IT WILL WORK OUT

In the end, He will 'work
everything together for good' and
for His glory.

1 Corinthians 10:31

RELAX

Soothing music has always had a
reputation for healing, tranquillising the distressed
and energising the weak. Listen to something
uplifting today
and receive a heart warming experience.

1 Samuel 16:23

LOOK BEYOND THE TRIAL

We are never closer to the Lord,
never more a recipient of His
strength than when trials come upon us.

Psalm 34:18
Psalm 145:18

OPEN UP TO JESUS

When you are hurting, you need
to declare it to the Lord. Remember He is
your Wonderful Counsellor.

Isaiah 9:6

SOMETHING BETTER WILL HAPPEN

Knowing that you have an eternal
inheritance and a secure home in Heaven ought to
help you rejoice through suffering.

James 2:5
John 14:1-3

REGRESS

Do something childish today, like going to the local park and swinging on the swings and sliding down the slide... it will soon get you giggling.

Mark 10:15

YOU'RE ONE OF A KIND.

You are of infinite worth
to God. His love for you is as though
you were the only one living in this world.

Psalm 8

YOU'RE NOT AN OUTCAST

God draws near to the helpless, the
undeserving, the destitute and all those who
simply feel they don't measure up.

Luke 15:1-2
Psalm 85:6

THINK HIGHLY OF YOURSELF IN GOD'S EYES

The next time you begin to think how unworthy
and irrelevant and useless you are, remember
that to God you are the object of
His attention and His affection.

Zechariah 2:8
Psalm 105:15

CHOOSE THE BEST

There is no comfort like God's
comfort.

2 Corinthians 1:3

BE DEPENDENT ON HIM

Faith is counting on Him when we
do not know what tomorrow holds.

Hebrews 11:1

YOU'RE SURROUNDED

God promises… 'I will go before you. I
will be on your right hand and on your left,
and my angels around about you, to bear you up.

Numbers 11:23
Matthew 4:6

SURPRISE YOURSELF

Watch out for those moments of surprised delights
like finding money in your coat from last winter.
Those pleasant surprises serve a purpose!

Isaiah 58:14

BE MORE WHOLE

Wounds cannot remain when the light
of God's love shines upon them. Absorb it and feel
its healing power.

Malachi 4:2

ENDURE

Expect troubles as an inevitable
part of life and repeat to yourself
the most comforting words of all: 'This too
shall pass.'

2 Samuel 1:1

TAKE A DEEP BREATH.

Fresh air gives you 66% of your energy.
Love the open air...it will give you fresh life
and zeal.

John 3:2

REMINISCE

Treasure the moments where you received love.
Those moments will survive long after
your money and good health has vanished.

Proverbs 10:7

LISTEN TO YOURSELF

The doctor within is on duty night and day,
working to keep you fit. Give this doctor a chance
now and then...listen to your body.

1 Corinthians 6:19

GAIN STRENGTH IN WEAKNESS

'The world breaks everyone, and afterwards many
are strong at the broken places.'

Ernest Hemingway

Psalm 34:18

TAKE A BREAK

More people complain of insomnia,
panic attacks and tension headaches than
ever before. Accept Christ's invitation…
'Come to me…and I will give you rest.'

Matthew 11:28

LOSE YOURSELF

An hour's solitude enables you
to think more clearly and
creatively. It's a sure path to comfort.

Zechariah 2:13

HOPE ON

We all need hope. It teaches us
that adversity does not last forever.

Matthew 5:10-12

BOUGHT WITH A PRICE

No one is insignificant in the
eyes of the Creator. What he
creates he cherishes.

Genesis 1:31
Genesis 1:26-28

KEEP MOVING

Don't give up when you are
just moments away from victory.
Your blessing may be just on the other side
of your problem.

Lamentations 3:25-26

HE'S ON YOUR CASE

'Weeping may endure for the night
but joy comes in the morning.' Be
encouraged. God is working in the dark!

Psalm 30:5

BELIEVE IN YOURSELF

When people reject you, it's usually
because they don't have the ability to see the
qualities inside you. They've bought into a lie.
Make sure you don't buy into it also!

Ezekiel 16:5-6

FREELY RECEIVE, FREELY GIVE

Until you care for yourself
you won't really be able to care
for anybody else. You can only give what
you allow yourself to receive.

Matthew 10:8

GOD KNOWS BEST

God knows you. He loves you and
He has a wonderful plan for your
life. When you can truly accept that,
your healing will begin.

Jeremiah 29:11

LET YOUR BLESSINGS OVERFLOW

Strive to leave a legacy that
enhances a positive memory and blesses
those you leave behind.

Psalm 112:6

STICK AT IT

Becoming a Christian is the work
of a moment. Learning to depend on
God is the work of a lifetime.
You're still a work in progress.

2 Corinthians 12:7-9

GROW FROM STRENGTH
TO STRENGTH

When you face tough times
and come through them, you develop
the faith needed to handle even tougher times.

Romans 12:3

SHARE YOUR PROBLEMS

Because you have a loving
Heavenly Father, whatever is important
to you is important to Him too.

Psalm 27:10

GO TO THE TOP

If you want real help, go to the
one who can give it. Jesus is
the problem-solver, direction-giver,
burden-bearer and the way-maker.

Genesis 18:14

BORN FOR A PURPOSE

Consider this:
You were born at just the right time
with just the right gifts to
fulfil a plan nobody else but you can
fulfil!

Psalm 139:14

PROTECTED 24/7

Not a single nagging,
aching, worrisome, gut-wrenching, blood pressure
rising thought escapes God's notice. You are His
personal concern.

1 Peter 5:7

GET OUT!

Walking is one of the best forms of
exercise. It puts a tingle in the blood,
promotes digestion, cleanses the mind and
elevates the spirit.

Jeremiah 6:16

SEEK GODLY ADVICE

The scriptures declare: 'Don't let the sun go
down on your anger.'
It's good advice.

Ephesians 4:26

WATCH FOR THE BLESSING

What you're struggling with right
now is part of your preparation. Get
ready – what the enemy meant for evil,
God's about to turn it for good.

Genesis 50:50

THE THIRD PERSON

Jesus promised before he returned to Heaven that
the Comforter would come – the Holy Spirit.
For this reason we are never left comfortless.

John 14:6

TRUST GOD'S PROCESS

To experience true comfort is
to sincerely believe that despite
what you're going through, everything will
eventually be OK.

2 Corinthians 13:11

COMFORT SOMEONE

The mere act of comforting someone
has reciprocal effects.
To comfort is to be comforted.

Isaiah 40:1
1 Thessalonians 4:18

THE WONDERFUL COUNSELLOR

The only one person who can
comfort you the way you need to be
comforted is God. He is the God of comfort.

Psalm 34:18
2 Corinthians 1:3-5

Other books by Richard Daly available from
Collins

God's little book of Calm

God's little book of Peace

God's little book of Love

God's little book of Hope

God's little book of Joy

www.collins.co.uk